The ANCIENT CHINESE

MYTHS of the WORLD

THE ANCIENT CHINESE

• VIRGINIA SCHOMP

MARSHALL CAVENDISH • BENCHMARK
NEW YORK

~ *For Desirae Autumn Thompson* ~

The author would like to thank Edward L. Shaughnessy, Creel Distinguished Service Professor of Early China, Department of East Asian Languages and Civilizations, the University of Chicago, for his valuable comments and careful reading of the manuscript.

Benchmark Books Marshall Cavendish 99 White Plains Road Tarrytown, New York 10591 www.marshallcavendish.us Text copyright © 2010 by Marshall Cavendish Corporation Map copyright © 2010 by Mike Reagan All rights reserved. No part of this book may be reproduced or utilized in any form or by any means electronic or mechanical, including photocopying, recording, or by any information storage and retrieval system, without permission from the copyright holders. All Internet sites were available and accurate when this book was sent to press. LIBRARY OF CONGRESS CATALOGING-IN-PUBLICATION DATA Schomp, Virginia. The ancient Chinese / Virginia Schomp. p. cm. — (Myths of the world) Includes bibliographical references and index. Summary: "A retelling of several important ancient Chinese myths, with background information describing the history, geography, belief systems, and customs of the people of China"—Provided by the publisher. ISBN 978-0-7614-4216-5 1. Mythology, Chinese—Juvenile literature. I. Title. BL1825.S34 2009 299.5´1113—dc22 2008034954

EDITOR: Joyce Stanton   ART DIRECTOR: Anahid Hamparian
PUBLISHER: Michelle Bisson   SERIES DESIGNER: Michael Nelson

Images provided by Rose Corbett Gordon, Art Editor of Mystic CT, from the following sources: Cover: The Art Archive/Musée Guimet Paris/Gianni Dagli Orti Back cover: Werner Forman/Art Resource, NY Pages 1, 23, 65, 67: Werner Forman/Art Resource, NY; pages 2–3: Doug Landreth/Corbis; pages 6, 12, 41, 74, 79: Werner Forman Archive/Topham/The Image Works; pages 7, 15, 58, 71, 76, 78, 84, 90 bottom: Artkey/Corbis; pages 8, 48, 59, 68, 70, 89 bottom: Asian Art & Archaeology, Inc./Corbis; pages 10–11: Museum of Fine Arts, Boston/Special Chinese and Japanese Fund/Bridgeman Art Library; pages 16, 18: Panorama/The Image Works; page 19: The Art Archive/National Palace Museum Taiwan; page 22: The Art Archive/Topkapi Museum Istanbul/Gianni Dagli Orti; pages 24, 26: Snark/Art Resource, NY; page 28: Bibliotheque des Arts Decoratifs, Paris, Archives Charmet/Bridgeman Art Library; page 30: The Art Archive/Private Collection Paris/Gianni Dagli Orti; pages 32–33: Calke Abbey, Derbyshire, UK/Mark Fiennes/Bridgeman Art Library; pages 34, 36: Historical Picture Archive/Corbis; page 37: The Art Archive/Nelson Atkin's Museum Kansas/Harper Collins Publishers; page 38: PoodlesRock/Corbis; pages 39, 75, 88 top: Private Collection/Bridgeman Art Library; pages 40, 57, 60, 62: The Granger Collection, NY; pages 42, 44, 88 bottom: Art Resource, NY; page 46: The Art Archive/Tokyo National Museum/Laurie Platt Whitney; page 47: The Art Archive/Claude Debussy Centre St. Germain en Laye/Gianni Dagli Orti; page 49: Réunion des Musées Nationaux/Art Resource, NY; pages 51, 52, 54, 89 top: SEF/Art Resource, NY; pages 56, 63 top: Christie's Images/Corbis; page 63 bottom: Blue Lantern Studio/Corbis; page 72: FuZhai Archive/Bridgeman Art Library; page 82: The Art Archive/British Museum; page 86: Victoria & Albert Museum/Art Resource, NY; page 87: Werner Forman Archive/Private Collection/The Image Works.

Printed in Malaysia
135642

Front cover: A silk painting of a bodhisattva, a Buddhist deity worshipped in ancient China
Half-title page: An elegant lady on a balcony, from an eighteenth- or nineteenth-century Chinese painting
Title page: The mountains alongside the scenic Li River almost seem to touch heaven itself.
Back cover: A tomb figure of a turtle, symbol of stability and long life

CONTENTS

THE MAGIC *of* MYTHS

EVERY ANCIENT CULTURE HAD ITS MYTHS. These timeless tales of gods and heroes give us a window into the beliefs, values, and practices of people who lived long ago. They can make us think about the BIG QUESTIONS that have intrigued humankind down through the ages: questions about human nature, the meaning of life, and what happens after death. On top of all that, myths are simply great stories that are lots of fun to read.

What makes a story a myth? Unlike a narrative written by a particular author, a myth is a traditional story that has been handed down from generation to generation, first orally and later in written form. Nearly all myths tell the deeds of gods, goddesses, and other divine beings. These age-old tales were once widely accepted as true and sacred. Their primary purpose was to explain the mysteries of life and

Above: Rooftops peek out from the trees in a majestic Chinese landscape.

the origins of a society's customs, institutions, and religious rituals.

It is sometimes hard to tell the difference between a myth and a heroic legend. Both myths and legends are traditional stories that may include extraordinary elements such as gods, spirits, magic, and monsters. Both may be partly based on real events in the distant past. However, the main characters in legends are usually mortals rather than divine beings. Another key difference is that legends are basically exciting action stories, while myths almost always express deeper meanings or truths.

Mythology (the whole collection of myths belonging to a society) played an important role in ancient cultures. In very early times, people created myths to explain the awe-inspiring, uncontrollable forces of nature, such as thunder, lightning, darkness, drought, and death. Even after science began to develop more rational explanations for

these mysteries, myths continued to provide comforting answers to the many questions that could never be fully resolved. People of nearly all cultures have asked the same basic questions about the world around them. That is why myths from different times and places can be surprisingly similar. For example, the people of almost every ancient society told stories about the creation of the world, the origins of gods and humans, and the afterlife.

A woman hangs harvested corn ears to dry outside her village home.

Mythology's other roles have included providing instruction, inspiration, and entertainment. Traditional tales offered a way for the members of a society to express their fundamental beliefs and values and pass them down to future generations. The tales helped preserve memories of a civilization's past glories and held up examples of ideal human qualities and conduct. Finally, these imaginative stories have provided enjoyment to countless listeners and readers from ancient times through today.

The MYTHS OF THE WORLD series explores the mythology of some of history's greatest civilizations. Each book opens with a brief look at the culture that created the myths, including its geographical setting, political history, government, society, and religious beliefs. Next comes the fun part: the stories themselves. We have based our retellings of the myths selected for these books on a variety of tradi-

Above: The mythical, magical Monkey King turns the hairs of his body into warriors.

tional sources. The new versions are fun and easy to read. At the same time, we have strived to remain true to the spirit of the ancient tales, preserving their magic, their mystery, and the special ways of speech and avenues of thought that make each culture unique.

As you read the myths, you will come across sidebars, or text boxes, highlighting topics related to each story's characters or themes. The sidebars in *The Ancient Chinese* include quoted passages from texts dating back hundreds or thousands of years. The sources for the excerpts are given in the Notes on Quotations on page 94. You will find lots of other useful material at the back of the book as well, including information on Chinese mythological texts, a glossary of difficult terms, suggestions for further reading, and more. Finally, the stories are illustrated with both ancient and modern paintings, drawings, and other works of art inspired by mythology. These images can help us better understand the spirit of the myths and the way China's traditional tales have influenced other cultures through the ages.

Now it is time to begin our adventures in ancient China. We hope that you will enjoy this journey to a land of powerful gods and spirits, superhuman heroes, and awe-inspiring dragons. Most of all, we hope that the sampling of stories and art in this book will inspire you to further explorations of the magical world of mythology.

A NOTE ON LANGUAGE

Scholars have used many different systems of spelling when translating Chinese words into English. In 1979 the government of the People's Republic of China adopted a new standard spelling system called pinyin. In most cases this book follows that system. We have included pronunciation guides for some especially difficult words.

Part 1

MEET *the* ANCIENT CHINESE

At the CENTER of THE WORLD

CHINA IS ONE OF THE LARGEST COUNTRIES IN THE world. Covering nearly 4 million square miles in eastern Asia, it is roughly the size of the United States and slightly smaller than Canada. Within this vast area are a great variety of landscapes. There are towering mountains, rocky plateaus, rolling hills, grasslands, steppes, deserts, narrow coastal plains, and fertile river valleys.

China's climate is as varied as the land. Temperatures in the country's many different regions range from sizzling hot to freezing cold and everything in between. During the winter months, dry winds flow out from the heart of Asia, bringing drought to most of the land. In the summer, warm moist winds blow inland from the Pacific Ocean. These monsoon winds bring heavy rains to much of the east.

Most of China's early settlers lived in the eastern part of the country. Temperatures in this area are generally milder than in the west. The land is mostly rolling hills and plains, watered by two great rivers:

Opposite: A man stands beside one of the thousands of rivers that crisscross the Chinese landscape.

Previous page: Court ladies prepare newly woven silk, in an early twelfth-century scroll painting.

CHINA AT THE TIME OF CONFUCIUS, AROUND 500 BCE

QIN EMPIRE 221–206 BCE

BORDER OF MODERN CHINA

CHINA

TIBET

INDIA

ZHUOLU

MOUNT TUSHAN

YELLOW SEA

EAST CHINA SEA

PACIFIC OCEAN

HUANG HE (YELLOW RIVER)

CHANG JIANG (YANGTZE RIVER)

GOBI DESERT

SILK ROAD

KUNLUN MOUNTAINS

HIMALAYAS

MILES

0   200   400

In the springtime the skies over China are filled with mallard ducks and other migrating birds.

the Huang He (also called the Yellow River) and the Chang Jiang (or Yangtze River). The fine soil deposited by these rivers fertilizes the surrounding lands, making the river valleys good places for farming.

Early settlers also enjoyed the protection of natural geographical barriers. To their east was the seemingly endless sea. To their north, south, and west were forbidding mountains, plateaus, steppes, and deserts. These land features tended to separate China from the rest of the world.

From time to time, people from other ancient civilizations managed to reach China by land or sea routes. The Chinese people sometimes borrowed new ideas and technologies from these foreign visitors. For the most part, though, they developed their own way of life in isolation. They regarded themselves as a people specially chosen by the gods and dismissed those of other cultures as uncivilized "barbarians." That attitude was reflected in a name they sometimes gave their homeland. They called it Zhongguo, which means "Central States" or "Middle Kingdom," because they believed that it was the center of the civilized world.

From VILLAGE to EMPIRE

THE HISTORY OF THE MIDDLE KINGDOM DATES BACK AT least seven thousand years. The earliest human settlements in what would become China were small farming villages along the banks of the Yellow and Yangtze rivers. Over the centuries those settlements grew into a number of different states. Rival states often fought over the control of territory. The kings of the strongest states ruled over the lands and people they conquered. Powerful families passed down control of their kingdoms from generation to generation. Chinese history is divided into periods named for these ruling families, or dynasties.

According to legend, the Xia (pronounced shah) family founded China's first dynasty. However, the Xia left few if any lasting traces of their civilization. The earliest dynasty for which we have solid evidence is the Shang, who came to power sometime around 1700 BCE. The Shang people made elaborately decorated bronze vessels. They also developed the earliest known system of Chinese writing, using inscriptions on turtle

Opposite: Houses were often built on stilts in marshy and flood-prone parts of China.

shells and ox bones to ask questions of the gods and ancestor spirits.

Around 1050 BCE the Zhou (joh) family overthrew the Shang. The Zhou controlled the Middle Kingdom for more than eight centuries. Their reign was marked by great political, scientific, and cultural advances. It ended in a time of war and upheaval known as the Warring States period. During that chaotic period, the lords of the seven largest Zhou states fought a series of bloody battles for supremacy.

In 221 BCE the state of Qin (chin) triumphed over all the others. The king of Qin took a new title: Shi Huangdi (shir hwong-dee), or "First Emperor." The dynasty founded by Qin Shi Huangdi marked the beginning of a new era, when all the land was united under a single ruler. It also gave us our name for that land, *China*.

The Qin dynasty collapsed after the death of its powerful leader. For the next four hundred years, the Han dynasty ruled China. Han emperors expanded the country's borders through diplomacy and war.

The wedding of a Chinese emperor was a grand and costly spectacle.

The DYNASTIES of IMPERIAL CHINA

Xia (uncertain) about 2205–1700 BCE

Shang about 1700–1050 BCE

Western Zhou about 1050–771 BCE

Eastern Zhou about 771–221 BCE

Warring States period about 475–221 BCE

Qin 221–206 BCE

Han 206 BCE–220 CE

Period of Division 220–581 CE

Sui 581–618 CE

Tang 618–907 CE

Five Dynasties period 907–960 CE

Song 960–1279 CE

Yuan 1279–1368 CE

Ming 1368–1644 CE

Qing 1644–1912 CE

Above: Taizong, second emperor of the Tang dynasty

They encouraged scholarship, science, technology, and the arts. They opened up trade with the outside world along a long overland route known as the Silk Road.

In 220 CE the Han dynasty dissolved into rival kingdoms. The land was divided for more than three hundred years. Then several dynasties followed, including the Sui, Tang, Song, Yuan, Ming, and Qing. Altogether the age of emperors lasted more than two thousand years, until the establishment of the Republic of China in 1912. During that long imperial age, the Chinese people created some of the world's largest cities and most ambitious engineering projects. They made advances and inventions in science and technology. They also created fine art and literature, including a treasure trove of myths that continue to entertain millions of people in China and around the world.

A variety of systems of dating have been used by different cultures throughout history. Many historians now prefer to use BCE (Before Common Era) and CE (Common Era) instead of BC (Before Christ) and AD (Anno Domini), out of respect for the diversity of the world's peoples.

The SOCIAL PYRAMID

THE EMPEROR STOOD AT THE VERY TOP OF ANCIENT Chinese society. The Chinese people honored their emperors as "Sons of Heaven"—extraordinary mortals whose mandate, or right to rule, came directly from the gods. That divine gift brought great power, along with grave responsibilities. As the head of the government, the emperor was responsible for ensuring the safety and prosperity of the empire. He also presided over religious rituals and sacrifices honoring the gods and the powerful spirits of his ancestors. If he failed to perform any of his duties properly, the gods could withdraw their mandate, and a new dynasty would rise.

Beneath the emperor was a privileged class of nobles and government officials. The noble class included the emperor's relatives and members of other important families. Government officials were organized by rank in a highly efficient administrative system. The highest-ranking officials worked in the imperial capital, advising the emperor and running the

government departments. Other ministers enforced the central government's laws and policies in provinces outside the capital.

The great majority of China's people were peasant farmers. Government decrees honored members of this class for providing the food and labor that were the backbone of the economy. Despite their high official status, peasants were the most downtrodden members of society. They worked long hours in the sun, wind, and rain. A flood or drought could wipe out an entire year's harvest. In both good years and bad, they had to pay taxes in the form of grain and labor. Farmers who could not pay their debts could lose their land. Some were even forced to sell their children into slavery.

Two high-ranking officials of a Ming dynasty court

Like farmers, craftspeople were considered productive members of society. China's skilled craftspeople produced practical goods such as clay pots and sturdy iron tools and weapons. They also turned out luxury items, including fine jewelry, beautifully patterned silk, and exquisite bronze and lacquered vessels.

Merchants took last place on the social scale. Buying and selling the goods that other people made was considered a dishonorable

Elegant ladies at an imperial feast. The woman on the left is playing a string instrument called a *pipa*, while her partner plays a small flute.

occupation. The lowly status of merchants did not prevent some of them from gaining wealth and influence. The son of a successful trader might become a government official, while his daughter might marry into a noble family.

Wives of all classes were expected to be humble and submissive to their husbands. Despite these restrictions, women of the upper class often enjoyed considerable respect and authority within their homes. At the imperial court, women influenced important decisions, including the choice of the emperor's heir. During the Tang dynasty, one forceful woman named Wu Zetian even became a "Son of Heaven" in her own right.

A BLENDING *of* FAITHS

THE RELIGION OF IMPERIAL CHINA WAS A BLENDING OF ancient beliefs and the teachings and stories of three later faiths: Confucianism, Taoism, and Buddhism.

Traditional beliefs: China's earliest people worshipped a multitude of divine beings. The gods of nature were everywhere—in trees, mountains, rivers, the sky, the stars, the thunder. They brought rainfall and drought, health and sickness, victory and defeat. The spirit world was also home to many ancestor spirits. The ancestors of kings and other important people had especially godlike powers.

Confucianism: The Chinese wise man and teacher Confucius was born in the sixth century BCE, during a period of great political and social unrest. In response to his chaotic times, he developed a system of ideas that called for a society based on order and morality. After his

Opposite: The Chinese wise man Kong Fuzi, known in the West as Confucius

death the philosophy known as Confucianism became the foundation of China's highly structured government. While Confucianism was not strictly a religion, it had a major impact on religious practices and mythology. Confucius stressed the importance of observing the proper rituals for honoring the ancestors. His followers collected and recorded the ancient stories of mythical god-kings.

Taoism (or Daoism): Around the same time that Confucius was teaching, other philosophers were developing the basic ideas of Taoism (DOW-izm). According to tradition, the father of Taoism was

According to legend, Laozi grew weary of the evils of humankind and rode off into the desert to escape society.

Laozi (low-zuh), also known as Lao-tzu. This wise man recorded his beliefs in the *Tao De Jing*, or "The Classic of the Way and the Power." The *Tao De Jing* urged people to live a simple life, in harmony with the flow of nature. That would lead them to the Tao, or "Way," which was the mystical source of all being. Over the centuries Taoism developed into a complex combination of religion and philosophy, embracing many different mystical practices. Some followers used special diets, exercises, and "magic potions" in attempts to gain immortality and supernatural powers.

Buddhism: Buddhism came to China from India during the first century CE, through travelers along the Silk Road. This ancient faith had been founded centuries earlier by the Indian prince Siddhartha Gautama, also known as the Buddha, or "Enlightened One." The Buddha taught that people are reborn, or reincarnated, many times. He outlined a path to salvation based on a set of strict moral guidelines. Virtuous people who followed this path would eventually achieve release from the cycle of rebirth, entering a state of endless bliss called nirvana. Over time the Chinese people added the divine beings of Buddhism to their vast family of deities. They also adopted many Buddhist beliefs, including ideas about reincarnation and an underworld where souls were judged before returning to life in their new bodies.

In **TOUCH** *with the* **HEAVENLY EMPIRE**

THE LIVES OF THE ANCIENT CHINESE REFLECTED THEIR country's unique blending of religious beliefs and practices. A family might worship the ancient gods through the religious rituals prescribed by Confucianism. They also might strive to follow Buddhism's moral principles and guidelines. At the end of a long day, they might surround themselves with the beauty of nature, finding peace of mind in Taoism's mystical Way.

The day-to-day religious practices of most Chinese focused mainly on practical concerns. Every home had an altar where the family presented offerings to the spirits of their ancestors. In return, the dead watched over the living, bringing guidance and good fortune. The Chinese also honored a host of local gods and guardian spirits. They pasted paper images on their front doors, representing the two guardians who prevented evil spirits from entering. They burned incense before images of the gods who safeguarded the back entrance,

Opposite: A father and son pay their respects at their family's ancestral altar.

This richly dressed priest may have served in a Taoist temple during the Song dynasty.

courtyard, and other parts of the house. They visited shrines and temples to honor the deities responsible for the wind, the rain, the soil, wealth, happiness, and other aspects of the world.

All these gods and goddesses were organized in a heavenly administration modeled on the country's political system. Like their earthly counterparts, the lower-ranking gods had to make regular reports to their higher-ups. The god of the kitchen, for example, went up to heaven on the first day of each year to report on the members of the household. The family sent him off with a tasty meal, so that he would speak favorably about them. They might even offer the god's image a sticky treat, in the hopes that his mouth would stick shut.

China's priests were responsible for building and maintaining the shrines and temples. They presided over elaborate rituals honoring the major gods and spirits. They also practiced divination to interpret the signs of heaven's intentions. Diviners used methods such as throwing lots or "reading" the pattern of cracks on animal bones to receive messages from the gods and ancestors.

The chief priest was the emperor. As the "Son of Heaven," this exalted being had a special ability to communicate with the spirit world. Several of the stories that follow will take us back in time to the first emperors, the mythical beings who ruled over China at the very beginning of the world.

Part 2

TIMELESS TALES
of ANCIENT CHINA

THE ORIGINS *of the* WORLD *and* HUMANS

Pangu the Giant and Nü Gua the Serpent Goddess

THE ANCIENT CHINESE TOLD MANY DIFFERENT STORIES about the origins of the world and the first people. One of the most popular creation myths featured a giant named Pangu. According to this ancient tale, the universe was once a vast cloud of vapor, which was shaped like a giant egg. Born inside the "cosmic egg," Pangu proceeded to bring order out of chaos. First he broke the egg, allowing the vapor to take shape as the heavens and the earth. Then he pushed the sky and the earth far apart, so that they would never dissolve together again. Finally, when he died, his body was magically transformed into the natural features of the world.

The Pangu creation story introduces us to the important concept of yin and yang. According to traditional Chinese thought, everything in the world is made up of these two opposing but related forces. Yin is the "female" force, associated with darkness, cold, dampness, and submissiveness. Yang is "male," with characteristics that are bright, hot,

Opposite: Flowers, like these orchids, sprang up when the world was created.

Previous page: A golden dragon adorns Chinese embroidery. Dragons represented power, wisdom, and goodness.

dry, and dominant. When Pangu broke the cosmic egg, all the elements of creation separated into yin and yang, bringing about the ordering of the universe.

Some Chinese myths say that Pangu created not only the heavens and the earth but also the human race. Other tales give the credit for human creation to Nü Gua. This ancient goddess was a shape-shifter, a mythical being with the power to change into different forms. In her most common form, she was a serpent or dragon. At the beginning of the world, Nü Gua molded the first people from yellow earth. These perfectly formed men and women were the ancestors of the nobles who would rule over Chinese society. A later batch of humans, made quickly and carelessly from mud, would become the common people.

CAST *of* CHARACTERS

Pangu Creator of the universe
Nü Gua Goddess who created humankind
Fu Xi Mythical first emperor; brother-husband of Nü Gua

Pangu Creates the Sky and the Earth

LONG AGO, at the beginning of time, heaven and earth were mingled together. All was the same, in a vast empty universe. All was dim and misty, formless and endless, a swirling desolation.

It is said that this mass of confusion was shaped like a giant chicken's egg. At the heart of the egg, Pangu was born. Pangu was the

Pangu separated the sky and the earth, making room for all the natural features of the world.

first of all beings, the child of the forces of the universe.

For countless ages Pangu slept inside the egg. Finally, he woke up and stretched his arms. The shell of the egg cracked, and everything inside poured out. The light and pure parts that were yang floated up and became the sky. The dark and heavy parts that were yin sank down and became the earth.

Pangu was pleased with the separation of sky and earth, but he feared that they would not remain divided. So he stood with the blue sky resting on his head and his feet pressing down on the yellow earth. The sky rose higher, the earth sank deeper, and Pangu grew taller in the space between them.

For 18,000 years Pangu stood like a pillar. Each day the sky rose ten feet higher, and the earth sank ten feet deeper. Each day Pangu grew ten feet taller, until he had grown into an enormous giant.

At last the sky reached its highest height, and the earth reached its lowest depth. Pangu saw that the two were fixed firmly in place. Never again would the world dissolve into chaos.

The giant's right eye rose into the sky and became the first full moon.

Sighing with relief, the giant lay down to rest from his long labors. He breathed deeply one last time and drifted into a peaceful death. As he died, his breath was transformed into the wind and clouds. His voice became the rolling thunder. His left eye rose as the sun, his right eye as the moon. The hairs of his head and beard turned into the countless stars. The sweat of his brow streamed down as the life-giving rain.

The other parts of the giant's body became the features of the earth. His trunk and limbs turned into the sacred mountains of the five directions: north, south, east, west, and center. His flesh formed the fertile fields. His muscles and veins became the paths that humans would travel. The hairs on his body grew as the grass, plants, and trees. His blood flowed into the seas, lakes, and rivers. His teeth and bones became rock and metal, while the marrow of his bones hardened into precious pearls and jade. The dying body of Pangu even gave rise to living beings, when the tiny specks on his skin sprang forth as the fish and animals.

And so it was that the firstborn, Pangu the giant, brought order out of chaos and filled heaven and earth with all their splendors.

Nü Gua Creates the First People

When the earth was complete, Nü Gua came down from heaven to see the great creation. Nü Gua was a remarkable goddess who could change her shape at will. In her favorite form, she had the head of a woman and the body of a serpent.

Nü Gua slithered across the quiet landscape on her long tail. She saw the mountains, forests, and rivers. She saw the busy fish and animals. Everything was beautiful, but somehow the world still seemed dull and empty.

All alone, the goddess lay down on the bank of a deep, calm river. She gazed at her own reflection in the water. Suddenly she had an idea. She would use her divine powers to create some companions.

Nü Gua scooped up a handful of sticky yellow earth. She molded the clay into a small figure. Instead of a tail like her own, she gave her

The serpentine goddess Nü Gua was lonely in a world without people.

creation two legs, so that it could walk around on the face of the earth. When she was finished, she placed the first human being on the ground, and it began to dance with happiness.

What a delightful creature! Nü Gua made another figure and another. The perfect little men and women laughed and danced around their great mother, and the goddess was no longer lonely.

All through the day and night, Nü Gua labored feverishly to fill the world with her children. Finally she became too tired to finish the task.

NÜ GUA KNEADED YELLOW EARTH AND FASHIONED HUMAN BEINGS.

⌐2ND CENTURY CE CHINESE TEXT

She had to find a way to work more quickly and easily.

So the goddess plucked a length of vine from the riverbank. She dragged the vine through a muddy ditch. She cracked it in the air like a whip, flinging drops of mud all around her. As each clod touched the earth, it turned into a human being. That is why we have nobles and commoners. The rich and fortunate nobles were each carefully shaped by the goddess. Those who formed from the haphazardly flung drops of mud became the poor and humble people.

At last there were plenty of human beings. But people made from clay and mud could not live forever. What would happen when they grew old and died? After much thought the goddess came up with an answer to this dilemma. Calling the men and women together, she taught them how to marry and raise children. Now humans could create their own sons and daughters.

Fu Xi was the first divine emperor of the newly created human race.

In time Nü Gua herself took a husband. She married her brother Fu Xi, and he became the first emperor. The great god showered humankind with blessings. He showed the people how to hunt and fish. He taught them the arts of writing, divination, and making music. Fu Xi also gave humans the valuable gift of fire.

All the people honored Fu Xi and Nü Gua for their gifts. They built temples and sang the praises of their god and goddess. And for many long years, the men and women of the earth lived in peace and happiness.

NÜ GUA REPAIRS *the* SKY

The mother goddess Nü Gua not only created humans but also saved them from extinction after the world's first war. According to this ancient story, Gong Gong, a god of water, and Zhu Rong, a god of fire, fought over which was more powerful. Gong Gong lost the battle. In his fury he knocked down one of the four pillars that held up the corners of the sky. The sky shattered, the earth cracked, and fires, floods, and other calamities followed. An ancient Chinese text called *Huainanzi* ("Master Huai-nan") explains how Nü Gua patched up the sky and made new pillars from the legs of a giant turtle. *Huainanzi* was written by Taoist scholars around 140 BCE, during the early Han dynasty.

Long ago Gong Gong fought with Zhu Rong to be God. In his fury he knocked against Buzhou Mountain [the sacred mountain of the West]. The pillar of Heaven broke and the cord of earth snapped. . . .

Fires raged fiercely and could not be extinguished. Water rose in vast floods without abating. Fierce beasts devoured the people. . . . Then Nü Gua [melted] five-color stones to mend the blue sky. She severed the feet of a giant sea turtle to support the four poles. . . . And she piled up the ashes from burned reeds to dam the surging waters. The blue sky was mended. The four poles were set right. The surging waters dried up. . . . Fierce beasts died and the people of [earth] lived. . . .

When one considers her achievement, it knows only the bounds of Ninth Heaven above and the limits of Yellow Clod below. She is acclaimed by later generations, and her brilliant glory sweetly suffuses the whole world. . . . She holds the secret of the Way of the True Person and follows the eternal nature of Heaven and earth.

WARS *of the* GODS

The Yellow Emperor

ACCORDING TO MYTHOLOGY, THE FIRST THREE EMPERORS of China were gods who came to dwell on the earth. The names of these divine emperors vary in accounts from different time periods and regions. During the Han dynasty, the list commonly included Fu Xi (husband of the creator goddess Nü Gua), Shen Nong (a god of agriculture), and Huang Di, or the Yellow Emperor.

The Yellow Emperor may have been partly based on a real king or chief who lived in the Yellow River region thousands of years ago. After his death this leader was honored as a minor god. Over time he grew in importance, inspiring a host of myths. Beginning with the Qin dynasty, all of China's rulers took the title *Huangdi*, or "emperor," linking themselves with the Yellow Emperor and the other mythical god-kings.

Huang Di's fame derived largely from his role as a culture hero. A culture hero is a mythical character who gives the essential tools of civilization to humankind. Various stories credit the Yellow Emperor with

Opposite: The dragon was a symbol of imperial power. Clouds and waves connect this seventeenth-century figure to its two domains, sky and water.

giving the people of China gifts such as government and the pottery wheel. Han dynasty historians hailed him as the founder of Chinese culture and the ancestor of the Han people.

Ancient myths also portray the Yellow Emperor as a powerful warrior. Although he longs for peace, he is forced to fight against a series of enemies who challenge his authority. He defeats his rivals through his supernatural powers and his mastery over wild animals and water. Through his victories he restores the Taoist ideals of balance and harmony to the world.

CAST *of* CHARACTERS

Huang Di Mythical third emperor; also called the **Yellow Emperor**

Yan Di Brother of Huang Di; also called the **Flame Emperor**

Tai Hao God of the east

Shao Hao God of the west

Gao Yang God of the north

Chi You God of rain and war

Ba Daughter of Huang Di; goddess of drought

Ying Long A warrior dragon

Xing Tian A giant from southern China

A Battle of Brothers

LONG AGO, IN THE DAYS when gods still dwelled among humans, Huang Di, the Yellow Emperor, ruled over the Middle Kingdom. This great god loved peace, but he did not hesitate to go to war when his kingdom was threatened. "If a ruler is in danger, the people beneath him will feel troubled and uneasy," said the wise emperor. "If a ruler loses his kingdom, his officials will ally themselves with another, and their loyalties will be forever uncertain. No good king could ever allow such a threat to the harmony of his subjects."

The first threat to Huang Di's reign came from an unexpected source: the emperor's own brother, Yan Di. This jealous god commanded the forces of fire, and thus he was known as the Flame Emperor. The Yellow Emperor and the Flame Emperor each ruled over half the world. One day Yan Di decided that he no longer wanted to share his authority. He would overthrow his brother and become the world's sole ruler.

The two brothers gathered their forces. The Flame Emperor's army was made up of monsters and demons. The Yellow Emperor's ranks were filled out with bears, wolves, panthers, tigers, and other wild creatures. Shrieks and howls tore the sky as the savage warriors met on the northern plains of Zhuolu. Hundreds were killed or wounded. The blood flowed in ghastly streams across the battlefield. Still, at the end of a long day of fighting, neither side had proven victorious.

That was when the Flame Emperor called up his greatest weapon. With a cry of rage, he hurled blazing shafts of fire at his brother's army. The Yellow Emperor responded with his own divine weapon: water. Towering waves met the flames and quenched them completely. The Flame Emperor's forces were defeated, and Yan Di himself was captured.

Following his great victory, Huang Di established order throughout the universe. He appointed four gods to watch over the four directions. The Four Emperors were Tai Hao in the east, Shao Hao in the west, Gao Yang in the north, and Yan Di, the defeated Flame Emperor, in the south.

Chief of all these gods was Huang Di. The Yellow Emperor built a magnificent jade palace at the top of Mount Kunlun. There he reigned as the god of the center and the supreme ruler of heaven and earth.

Yan Di, the Flame Emperor, was appointed god of the south.

The War God's Rebellion

Many officials served the Yellow Emperor at the imperial court. Among these was Chi You, god of rain and war. With his massive iron head, sharp horns, and cloven hooves, Chi You was a fearsome sight. His seventy-two brothers, who lived in a village in the south, were just as huge and powerful. These brutish brothers were blacksmiths whose specialty was making iron spears, swords, and other weapons of war.

Although Chi You was just a minor official, he had an arrogance to match his bull-like appearance. He was convinced that he was stronger and smarter than the Yellow Emperor. Eager to prove his might, he

The Yellow Emperor conquered his brother's fire with the divine weapon of water.

plotted to overthrow Huang Di and seize the throne. Traveling to the south, he rallied his brothers and recruited a tribe of barbarians to join his rebellion. Then he led his troops north, toward the imperial capital.

Word of the approaching army soon reached the Jade Palace. The peace-loving emperor sent messengers to try to reason with Chi You, but the rebel leader was too consumed with ambition to listen. So once again Huang Di summoned the bears, wolves, tigers, and other wild animals. His troops sallied forth from the capital and met the enemy army at the famous battlefield of Zhuolu.

Swords, spears, and battle-axes clashed. Teeth and claws dripped with blood. The two armies were equally matched. But Chi You was prepared to try any trick to overcome his opponent. At the height of the fighting, the bull-headed god used his magical powers to surround Huang Di's army with a thick white fog. The emperor's troops circled around blindly

as the enemy slashed and stabbed at them. Only the quick thinking of one of the imperial ministers saved the helpless army from total destruction. In a flash the clever official created the first compass. With the help of this marvelous instrument, Huang Di and his troops found their way out of the deadly cloud.

Chi You was enraged by the emperor's escape. With a roar he summoned two of his allies, the masters of wind and rain. The divine pair unleashed a terrible storm, driving back the Yellow Emperor's army.

The homely old goddess Ba was also called Drought Fury, for her power to dry up the earth.

Huang Di was surveying the battle from a hilltop. When he saw that his troops were in trouble, he called for his daughter Ba. This goddess was old and ugly, but she had one special power: she could store scorching heat in her body. At her father's command, Ba walked out onto the storm-whipped battlefield. The heat of her body forced the winds to flee and dried up the rains.

The emperor had won the battle, but the war was not over yet. As the fighting dragged on, his troops were becoming more and more weary. Huang Di knew that he needed something to lift his warriors' spirits and dishearten the enemy. At last he came up with an idea. He would make the world's first war drum.

The emperor sent his strongest warriors to the Eastern Sea*, where they captured and killed a roaring water monster. He sent another company of soldiers to the mountain home of a powerful thunder dragon.

*Mythological texts use the name "Eastern Sea" for the East China Sea and Yellow Sea, two arms of the Pacific Ocean.

The two groups returned with their prizes: the hide of the sea monster and the two largest bones from the dragon. They stretched the hide over a barrel. The gigantic bones would serve as drumsticks.

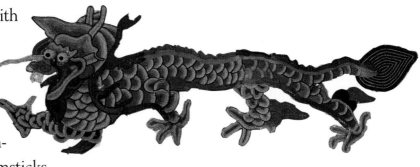

Now the emperor led his army back into battle. He raised the dragon bones and struck the war drum nine times. The thunderous sound echoed for five hundred leagues, making the

> ## IN THE EASTERN SEAS THERE IS A BEAST. . . . ITS VOICE IS LIKE THUNDER.
> *⌐THE CLASSIC OF MOUNTAINS AND SEAS*

mountains sway and the valleys tremble. Chi You's soldiers cowered in terror. The Yellow Emperor's forces rushed in and slaughtered more than half the rebel warriors.

Chi You and his remaining troops were surrounded on the field of battle. The war drum thundered. The emperor's divine dragon Ying Long swooped down, devouring the enemy. The rebel army was completely wiped out, and the rebel leader was captured.

In sorrow Huang Di condemned his former minister to death. Only Ying Long had the courage to carry out the sentence. With one quick slash of his sharp claws, the dragon cut off the head of the powerful war god. The bloody chains from Chi You's wrists were hurled out into the wilderness. On the spot where they landed, the first maple trees grew. Each year the leaves of these trees turn red, as an everlasting reminder of Chi You's punishment.

Huang Di Joins the Immortals

After the death of Chi You, the Yellow Emperor faced two more challenges to his authority. First he had to fight a giant named Xing Tian, who wanted to rule over the earth and heaven. That fierce battle ended when the emperor lopped off the giant's head and hid it inside a mountain. Next the emperors of the four directions rose up against their supreme ruler. With a sigh, Huang Di called up his army and demolished them.

That final victory marked the end of the wars of the Yellow Emperor. From then on, Huang Di presided over an era of peace and prosperity in which all people lived in harmony with nature. In this happy age, the emperor gave the people of the earth many gifts to make their lives better. He divided the earth into territories and introduced strictly ordered systems of law and government. He created the first boats and carts, the pottery wheel, the calendar, coins, and medicine. He taught the people how to plant their crops in season and cook their food before eating it.

Altogether Huang Di ruled for one hundred years. At the end of his long reign, he rode up to heaven on the back of a golden dragon. Many members of the emperor's household joined him as he went to dwell among the immortals. Sadly, two divine beings were left behind. Ba, who had helped her father defeat the war god Chi You, was too exhausted to make the journey to heaven. She was forced to remain among humans, an unwelcome visitor who brought heat and drought wherever she wandered. Ying Long the dragon also remained on the earth. He traveled south to live among the high peaks and mountain pools. To this day the dragon's breath still brings rain to the south of China.

The Yellow Emperor taught his people many skills, including the making of pottery.

THE ADVENTURES
of a HERO

Yi the Archer and the Ten Suns

MANY ANCIENT PEOPLES TOLD STORIES ABOUT THE adventures of heroes who used their superhuman skills, strength, and courage to help humankind. One of the most popular mythical heroes of ancient China was the divine archer Yi. This contradictory character appears in a number of different myths. In some tales he is a villain whose crimes include the overthrow of the legendary Xia dynasty. More often, though, Yi is remembered as the hero who saved the world from the catastrophe of the ten suns.

According to the ancient tale, there were once ten boy-suns (one for each day of the week in the ancient Chinese calendar). The boys normally took turns appearing in the sky. One day they decided to come out all at once, and the world was nearly incinerated. Their father, an early god known as Di Jun, sent Yi the archer to chase his sons out of the sky. Consumed with anger over the earth's suffering, Yi exceeded his orders, shooting and killing nine of the suns. He then

Opposite: The divine hero Yi wielded a bow and arrow, just like this eighteenth-century Chinese emperor.

went on a heroic quest to rid the world of monsters. The bowman's deeds restored peace and order to the world. However, Di Jun was furious over the slaying of his sons. The god stripped the divine archer of his immortality and condemned him to live and die on the earth.

The dramatic story of Yi and the ten suns is set in the days of the mythical emperor Yao. Yao was the fourth ruler after the Yellow Emperor, the main character in our last story. He was also the first of three mythical Sage Kings, who presided over a Golden Age of perfect government. Confucius and his followers pointed to Emperor Yao as an example of the ideal king, because he ruled with virtue, justice, and devotion to his subjects.

CAST *of* CHARACTERS

Di Jun Father of the ten suns; early god of the eastern sky
Xi He Mother of the ten suns; a sun goddess
Yao Mythical seventh emperor; first of the three Sage Kings
Yi Divine archer
Chang E Wife of Yi; a moon goddess

BEYOND THE EASTERN SEA there is an island. On the island stands a giant mulberry tree. This tree is so tall that its top reaches the heavens. It is so broad that a thousand men standing with outstretched arms could not encircle its trunk.

Ten playful suns once lived among the branches of this marvelous tree. The boys were the sons of Di Jun, god of the eastern sky, and his divine wife, Xi He. Each morning Xi He would drive up to the tree in a chariot pulled by six flying dragons. She would pick up one of her sons, and together they would ride to the eastern edge of the sky. All day the golden chariot would soar across the heavens, and the sun would light up the earth. By the time the chariot dipped below the western mountain, the weary boy-sun would be sleeping. The goddess would fly back to the mulberry tree, give her children their baths, and tuck them into bed among the leafy branches.

After a few hundred years, the ten suns grew tired of this routine. They did not want to wait their turn to ride in their mother's chariot. They wanted to play in the sky together! So one morning, before Xi He arrived, all the boy-suns flew up from the tree. They sang and danced among the clouds. They laughed when they heard their mother calling. They had such a good time that they vowed they would never again be parted.

While the boys were enjoying themselves in the sky, the people of the earth were suffering. They had watched in amazement as one sun after another rose over the eastern horizon. Their wonder had turned to horror as the ten bright suns began to dry up the soil and wither the crops in the fields. Soon the lakes and rivers were boiling. Even the rocks were melting. Wild animals and monsters fled the steaming forests and devoured hundreds of men, women, and children.

In their fear and despair, the people turned to Emperor Yao. The compassionate ruler prayed night and day, begging Di Jun to take pity on his wretched subjects. When the god heard the emperor's plea, he ordered his sons to stop their nonsense and return to the mulberry tree. But the unruly boys were having too much fun to pay attention to their father.

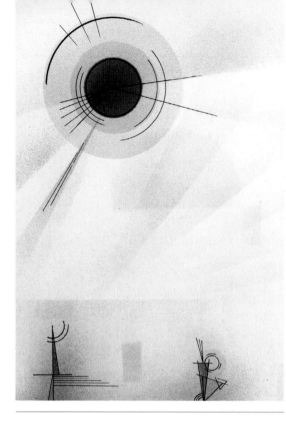

THE TEN SUNS ALL ROSE AT ONCE, SCORCHING THE SHEAVES OF GRAIN.
⌐HUAINANZI

So Di Jun sent for the immortal archer Yi. He gave the warrior a magnificent red bow and a quiver filled with white arrows. "Go down to the earth and reestablish order," Di Jun commanded. "Use this bow to frighten my sons into obedience."

In a flash Yi descended to the earth to obey the god's orders. He saw the scorched and blistering land. He saw the helpless people cowering in their huts, hungry, exhausted, and terrified. His heart filled with rage. The time for peaceful measures was past! The false suns must be destroyed, or all life on earth would perish!

Quickly Yi counted out ten arrows from his quiver. He drew his bow and fired. A white arrow streaked across the sky, and one of the suns fell to the earth in a ball of fire.

Again and again the hero unleashed his arrows. There were eight suns left. Seven. Six. The earth was becoming cooler. The people began to creep from their huts and cheer on their champion. But Emperor Yao was getting worried. Yi was so intent on his mission that Yao feared the hero would kill all the suns, plunging the earth into eternal darkness. Quietly the emperor ordered one of his soldiers to sneak up and steal one of the archer's arrows.

Now there was only one sun left. Yi reached for his last arrow. It was missing! The hero gazed up at the sky. He looked around at the cheering people. Slowly he lowered his bow. One sun would remain to give light and warmth to the earth.

Yi the divine archer had saved the world from disaster. But the people were still in danger. Without hesitation the hero took up his sword and filled his quiver with new arrows. Then he set out to battle the wild beasts and monsters.

For many long days, Yi traveled across the earth. He hunted down a man-eating monster called Chiseltooth, which shredded its victims with a huge tooth as sharp as the cutting edge of a chisel. Yi killed this bloodthirsty creature with a single arrow. Next he tackled the deadly Windbird, which whipped up destructive storms by flapping its gigantic wings. Yi tied a cord to an arrow and shot the bird in the chest. Then he dragged it down to the ground and beheaded it. Most fearsome of all was a gigantic sea serpent that was devouring the people of a lakeside village. Yi shot the serpent until its scaly hide bristled with arrows. He finally killed it by piercing its heart with his sword.

All these creatures and more the divine archer slew. When he had destroyed all the monsters, he drove the wild animals back into the forests. At last Yi's heroic labors were completed, and there was peace on the earth. All the people sang his praises, and Emperor Yao held a great feast in his honor.

Then the divine archer returned to heaven, where his wife, the goddess Chang

THE GREAT GOD . . .
GAVE YI THE ARCHER
A GIFT OF A VERMILION
[RED] BOW.
~THE CLASSIC OF
MOUNTAINS AND SEAS

E, was waiting impatiently. But when Yi presented himself at the court of Di Jun, the god lashed out in anger. "I ordered you to frighten my sons, not kill them!" Di Jun shouted. "For that I can never forgive you. From this day on, you are banished from heaven. Since you love the people of the earth so much, you can go live among them as a mortal."

So it was that Yi the archer lost his immortality. Along with the unhappy Chang E, he went to live on the earth. The hero spent the remainder of his days serving Emperor Yao and hunting in the forests. He also taught the people how to hunt with the bow, so that his archery skills would never be lost.

Yi showed the people how to hunt ferocious tigers and other wild beasts.

In time the once-immortal archer died, and his spirit joined the ghosts of other mortals in the underworld. But his deeds were never forgotten. People still tell stories about the hero who shot the nine suns and vanquished the monsters. In this way Yi the archer achieved his own version of immortality.

CHANG E ESCAPES *to the* MOON

One of the best-known characters associated with Yi the archer is his wife, Chang E (also called Heng O). After the couple was banished from heaven, Chang E refused to accept the loss of immortality. She nagged her husband until he agreed to visit an ancient goddess known as the Queen Mother of the West, who guarded the magical potion of eternal life. Yi returned home to share the potion with his wife, but the greedy Chang E took it all herself. Fearing her husband's anger, she fled to the moon, where she was changed into an ugly toad in punishment for her selfishness.

Like most Chinese myths, the story of Chang E has been pieced together from fragments scattered through a variety of ancient texts. This passage comes from *Chu xue ji*, or "Sources for Beginning Scholarly Studies," an encyclopedia of myths compiled by the Chinese scholar Xu Jian around 700 CE.

Yi asked the Queen Mother of the West for the drug of immortality. Yi's wife, Heng O, stole it and escaped to the moon. She was metamorphosed [transformed] on the moon and became the striped toad Ch'an-ch'u, and she is the essence of the moon.

Above: The beautiful Chang E flees to the moon, where she will spend eternity as an ugly striped toad.

RESHAPING THE FACE *of the* EARTH

Yu Conquers the Great Flood

ANCIENT PEOPLES ALL OVER THE WORLD TOLD STORIES about a great flood. To the Chinese people, flood myths were especially significant. Since prehistoric times, China's vast rivers, especially the Yangtze and Yellow rivers, have supplied fertile soil and life-giving water to farm fields. At the same time, the people living around the rivers have faced the threat of deadly floods. This ever-present danger is reflected in at least four different Chinese flood myths. Unlike similar stories from other cultures, these tales generally present floods as natural disasters rather than divine punishments for human sins.

The hero of the best-known Chinese flood myth is Yu the Great. Yu was the son of Gun, a rebellious god who tried but failed to save the people of the earth from the great flood. To accomplish his mission, Gun stole a magical substance known as "Swelling Soil" from the Supreme God in heaven. (This high god might also be called Tian Di, Shang Di, the Jade Emperor, or simply God). Gun was executed for

Opposite: Villagers plant rice in a flooded field in southern China.

his crime, but his spirit was miraculously reborn in his son, Yu.

Like the goddess Nü Gua in our earlier myth, Yu was a shape-shifter. He was born in the form of a dragon. He devoted his life to redeeming his father's name by completing the task that Gun had started. Yu contained the flood by creating rivers, hills, and mountains. He also invented the network of dams and canals that the ancient Chinese used to channel the waters. Throughout his labors he demonstrated the highest ideals of a hero: intelligence, strength, devotion to duty, and perseverance in the face of all obstacles.

When his heroic task was completed, Yu was rewarded with the kingship, becoming the third and last Sage King of the Golden Age. After his death the throne went to his son, Qi. That marked the beginning of the legendary Xia dynasty. It also provided a mythological explanation for the tradition of hereditary rule that would be followed by all the real-life dynasties to come.

CAST *of* CHARACTERS

Yao Mythical seventh emperor; first of the three Sage Kings
Gun Father of Yu
Supreme God Ruler of heaven
Zhu Rong God of fire
Yu Controller of the flood; last of the three Sage Kings
Qi Son of Yu
Shun Second of the three Sage Kings

Gun Battles the Flood

IN THE DAYS OF EMPEROR YAO, the earth was devastated by a great flood. First came the rains, beating down for days without end. The fields turned into lakes, and the crops rotted in the muddy waters. Then the rivers overflowed their banks, and the swollen tide surged into the towns and villages. Thousands of men, women, and children were drowned. Other people took refuge in mountain caves and treetops. The wretched survivors watched in despair as the waters kept rising, until it was impossible to tell where the land began and the broad brown sea ended.

Emperor Yao's heart filled with pain at the suffering of his subjects. He turned to the heavens for help, sending up his prayers and offerings night and day. At last the immortal Gun answered. Gun was a rebellious god with a reputation for disobeying orders, but he was also brave and compassionate. Descending to the earth, he wept at the scene of misery and turmoil. He wanted to help, but he had no idea how to get rid of the waters.

Just then, two curious creatures came along. One was a horned owl, the other a giant turtle. "Why do you look so worried?" the giant turtle asked.

"I want to contain the flood, but I do not know how to build the barriers," Gun answered.

"That is not so difficult. All you need is a magical substance called Swelling Soil. It looks just like ordinary dirt, but it will grow into any size and shape you desire." Looking around

The horned owl and the turtle told Gun the secret of the magical Swelling Soil.

nervously, the turtle went on in a whisper: "There is only one problem. Swelling Soil is the most treasured possession of the Supreme God in heaven, and he will never part with it."

No one knows how Gun managed to steal the Swelling Soil from the Supreme God. We only know that he succeeded. Soon he returned to the earth with a lump of the precious substance. He dropped the soil into the muddy waters. Suddenly great dams and mountains sprang up, dividing the endless sea into lakes. Fresh new dirt grew up on the bottom of the lakes, absorbing the waters. Patches of dry land began to appear. People emerged from the caves and treetops, hailing Gun as their savior.

There was one who was far from pleased with the hero's handiwork, however. In fact, the Supreme God was furious when he saw that Gun had stolen the Swelling Soil and meddled in the affairs of humans without permission. In his anger, the god sent Zhu Rong, lord of fire, to punish the rebel. The fire god pursued his quarry to the slopes of Feather Mountain, at the northern edge of the world. He killed Gun with a stroke of his divine knife. Then he took the divine soil back to heaven. The dams and mountains tumbled down, and the earth once again sank beneath the floodwaters.

From the Belly of the God

It is no easy thing to destroy an immortal. After Gun's execution his divine body lay on the slopes of Feather Mountain for three years without decaying. All that time the spirit that lingered in the body was growing into a new being. When the Supreme God heard of this marvel, he sent one of his officials to dispose of the rebel once and for all. The official flew down to the mountain and slit open Gun's belly with his sword. Out flew Yu the Great, in the form of a yellow dragon.

Yu was born with all of his father's knowledge, courage, and compassion. He was also virtuous and dependable, without any of Gun's rebellious spirit. The golden dragon flew straight up to heaven. He bowed low before the throne of the Supreme God and said, "O merciful god, the people of the earth are weary with long suffering. I beg you to give me the Swelling Soil, so that I may complete the work that my father started."

Yu was born in the form of a powerful golden dragon.

The great god was impressed by the dragon's humility. "Your wish is granted," he proclaimed. "You may have the divine soil with my blessings. Now go, and devote yourself diligently to the task of subduing the floods."

Joyfully Yu winged his way back down to the earth. He dropped tiny lumps of the magical soil into the waters. Up sprang a series of mountains and dams, holding back the floodwaters.

Yu knew that it was not enough to merely contain the flood. He must also control the course of the rivers, so that they would flow freely and safely to sea. Using his shape-shifting powers, he changed into the form of a man. Then he set out across the face of the earth. Everywhere he traveled, he created new channels for the rivers to follow. He dug down to lower the riverbeds. He carved out new rivers and

GOD [ALLOWED] YU TO SPREAD OUT THE SELF-REPLACING SOIL SO AS TO QUELL THE FLOODS.
—THE CLASSIC OF MOUNTAINS AND SEAS

built canals. He cut down trees, leveled hilltops, and tunneled through mountains. As he worked, he also had to battle all the dangerous monsters that had emerged from the floodwaters.

Yu labored at his difficult mission for years without stopping. The sun blistered his skin. His hands and feet became covered with calluses. His clothes grew ragged, his health failed, and his steps faltered. Somehow the hero found the strength to continue his labors on behalf of humanity.

The Birth of a Dynasty

When Yu was thirty years old, he began to think about taking a wife. It was then that the heavens sent him a sign. He was walking past the slopes of Mount Tushan when a white fox with nine tails scampered across his path. Yu remembered the words of an ancient prophecy: "He who sees the nine-tailed fox and marries the maiden of Tushan shall wear a crown." He hurried to the nearest village, where he met the daughter of the chief. The famous hero asked for the girl's hand in marriage, and she and her father gladly accepted.

But the marriage was not a happy one. Yu worked so hard that he hardly ever came home, even after his wife became pregnant with their first child. One day the lonely girl came looking for her husband. The shape-shifting god had transformed himself into a giant bear in order to gouge a hole through a mountain. When the wife saw the fearsome beast, she was so terrified that she turned to stone. Horrified, Yu cried out, "My child! Give me my child!" With a loud crack, the rock split open, revealing a newborn baby boy.

Yu named his son Qi, which means "cracked open." As the boy grew up, he helped his father with his work. Together the two traveled

After the task of controlling the flood was completed, people lived in harmony with the waters.

across the Middle Kingdom, taming the waters and bringing peace and order to the world.

After many years Yu's heroic labors were finally completed. The rivers flowed in their proper channels. New lands had been opened up, with rich black soil perfect for farming. The hero had even laid down roads connecting the nine provinces.

During the years that Yu had toiled, Yao had died and a new emperor, Shun, had taken the throne. Now Shun himself was an old man. It was time for him to name his successor. All the people rejoiced when the emperor chose the hero whose tireless devotion to duty had saved the world from the great flood.

Yu the Great ruled the Middle Kingdom with wisdom, virtue, and humility. Worn out from his long labors, he died after only eight years on the throne. His spirit returned to heaven, where it will dwell for all eternity. And on the earth, his son, Qi, became the second emperor of the great Xia dynasty.

A MYTH
of the STARS

The Weaver Maid and the Cowherd

LIKE MOST ANCIENT PEOPLES, THE CHINESE WERE fascinated by the stars. By the early fourth century BCE, Chinese astronomers had already identified more than eight hundred stars and grouped them into constellations. A variety of divine beings were associated with these heavenly bodies. The star deities played a constant role in human affairs. "Lucky stars" might reward worshippers with good health, love, marriage, prosperity, or success in examinations. Other stars could have an evil influence, bringing disease, madness, drought, or war.

One of the most popular and enduring Chinese star myths is the story of the goddess Zhi Nü, known as the Weaver Maid, and the mortal cowherd Niu Lang. In this ancient tale, the Weaver Maid represents the bright white star that people of the Western world call Vega, while Niu Lang is the star Altair. The goddess and the herdsman fall in love, but they are torn apart by the girl's father, the Supreme God

Opposite:
Zhi Nü and Niu Lang gaze longingly across the heavenly waters that divide them.

in heaven. The god condemns the couple to live on opposite sides of the Milky Way, known as the "Sky River" or "Silver River." Once a year the parted lovers are permitted to cross over the river on a magical bridge formed by magpies (black-and-white birds that often symbolize happiness).

Since the Han dynasty, this tale of true love has been celebrated in the annual festival of Qi Xi (chee shee), or "Seventh Night." On this special evening, single women and newly married wives made offerings of flowers, fruit, pastries, and other sweet treats to Zhi Nü and Niu Lang. Young girls prayed for the goddess to share her skills as they took part in weaving and needlework competitions. These age-old traditions are dying out in modern China. However, many Chinese still mark the Qi Xi Festival with stargazing. Peering up at the night sky, they look for Vega and Altair shining on either side of the Milky Way, with a third star forming a bridge between them.

CAST *of* CHARACTERS

Zhi Nü Goddess of weaving and spinning; also known as the Weaver Maid
Supreme God Ruler of heaven
Niu Lang Mortal cowherd; husband of the Weaver Maid

IN OLDEN DAYS THE SILVER RIVER flowed all the way from heaven down to the earth. On the eastern bank of the sparkling waters sat Zhi Nü the Weaver Maid, daughter of the Supreme God in heaven. Day after day Zhi Nü toiled over her spinning wheel, making silk thread so fine that it was nearly invisible. With her magic loom, she wove the thread into clouds, which she set free to rise up into the heavens. The lovely young maiden also fashioned the delicate robes that adorned the gods and goddesses.

On the opposite side of the river dwelled the humble cowherd Niu Lang. This young man was an orphan. When his parents died, his elder brother had claimed the best land for himself. All that was left for the younger boy was a hard patch of ground and one old ox. But the cowherd was a cheerful, industrious young man. He worked hard in his fields without complaining. He also took good care of his ox, making sure the faithful animal always had enough to drink and eat.

As the years passed, the cowherd began to get lonely. He longed to share his life with a wife and children. One day he was resting from his solitary labors when something astonishing happened. His ox began to speak! As it happened, this was no ordinary ox. He was really a deity who had somehow angered the Supreme God and had been exiled from heaven in punishment.

The magical ox told the lonely cowherd how to find his truelove.

"You have been kind to me," the animal told his young master. "In return I will ease your loneliness. There is a hidden place on the Silver River where the seven daughters of the high god come to bathe. Tomorrow I will take you there, and you will find a wife."

So the next morning the ox led the cowherd to a clear pool in a bend of the Silver River. The young man concealed himself in the thick plants and trees that surrounded the waterhole. Soon seven heavenly maidens descended from the sky. Shedding their celestial robes, the divine girls stepped into the water.

Never had the cowherd beheld such grace and beauty! For a moment he could only watch in wonder. Finally he stole out from hiding. Creeping up to the water's edge, he gathered up the clothes of the youngest and most dazzling maiden.

Just then, one of the sisters spotted the strange mortal. She let out a cry, and the frightened girls grabbed their robes and fled back to heaven. Only the seventh maiden was left trembling in the water.

The herdsman knelt down at the edge of the pool. "I mean you no harm," he said softly. "You are the most enchanting creature in the world. I beg you to marry me and put an end to my loneliness."

The goddess and the cowherd lived like ordinary mortals in a simple farming village.

The gentle words of the handsome young stranger touched the girl's heart. She had been lonely, too, working day after day at her weaving. Shyly she gave her consent. And that is how the immortal Weaver Maid came to marry a simple cowherd.

For several years Zhi Nü and Niu Lang lived together in happiness. The husband worked in the fields, while the wife tended to her weaving.

They were blessed with two children, a boy and a girl, and no one in their little house was ever lonely.

Then the goddess began to neglect her divine duties. Caring for her home and family was so much work that there was little time left for weaving. The clouds began to vanish from the sky. The robes of the gods and goddesses fell into tatters. Looking down from heaven, the Supreme God grew more and more angry. Finally the god sent a messenger to bring Zhi Nü back to the eastern side of the Silver River.

Niu Lang watched in horror as the divine messenger flew off with his wife. Desperately the young man ran after them. He followed Zhi Nü's cries to the banks of the Silver River. There he stopped in amazement. The river no longer flowed down to the earth. The Supreme God had raised its glittering waters to run across the face of the heavens.

Sad and weary, the herdsman returned home, where another loss awaited him. His faithful ox was lying down in its stall. "It is nearly time for me to die," said the aged animal. "When I am gone, you must cut off my skin. Its magical properties will carry you to heaven."

That night the ox died, and the cowherd carried out its final instructions. He skinned the animal and wrapped its tough hide around him like a cape. He balanced a carrying pole across his shoulders. He placed his two little children in the baskets hanging from the ends of the pole. Then he lifted his eyes and took off for the heavens.

Swiftly Niu Lang flew toward the Silver River. He saw Zhi Nü waiting tearfully on the eastern bank. But the Supreme God had no intention of allowing the mortal to reclaim his daughter. Reaching out his

> GOD IN HEAVEN . . . PUNISHED [WEAVER MAID] BY ORDERING HER TO RETURN TO THE EAST OF THE RIVER.
> —LUO YUAN, 12TH CENTURY CE

Each year the birds form a bridge in the heavens, uniting the parted lovers.

divine hand, the god turned the river into a raging torrent.

The husband wept as he stood on the western bank. There was no way to cross the broad, stormy waters. Suddenly his daughter spoke up from the basket: "Father, why don't we empty out the river?"

At once Niu Lang began to drain the river with a ladle. His son and daughter helped by scooping out water with their hands. When the Supreme God saw the family working so hard at their hopeless task, his stern heart softened. "Very well," he said to the herdsman, "you may visit my daughter for one night every year."

And so, on the seventh day of the seventh month each year, flocks of magpies fly up from the earth to form a bridge across the Silver River. The cowherd crosses the feathery bridge with his children, and the family is reunited. The rest of the year, the husband and wife remain on opposite sides of the sparkling waters. If you turn your eyes to the night sky, you will see them. The bright star on the east side is the Weaver Maid, tending to her weaving under the watchful eyes of her father. To the west sits the cowherd, with his small son and daughter beside him, waiting patiently to rejoin his beloved.

THE CHINESE SPEAK
The SKY VOYAGER

The myth of the Weaver Maid inspired a number of other stories about the Milky Way. One tale featured a character known as the Sky Voyager, who built a flying machine and took off to explore the heavens. The following account of that magical journey comes from a third-century CE text called *Bo wu zhi*, or "Record of Things at Large." The text mentions a real-life astronomer named Yen Chün-p'ing (also known as Yan Junping), who lived during the first century BCE. It also refers to the Draught Ox constellation, another name for Aquila (the constellation that contains the star of the cowherd). According to the astronomer, the Sky Voyager himself had been transformed into a star during his voyage, and the mysterious place that he visited in the sky was the Draught Ox constellation.

In olden days it was said that Sky River [the Milky Way] was connected to the sea. Nowadays there is a man [the Sky Voyager] who lives on a little island. Year after year in the eighth month, a floating raft comes and goes, and it never fails to pass by at the same time. The man had a wonderful idea—he erected a soaring compartment on the raft, packed provisions, boarded the raft, and left. . . . He went on for ten days or more, when suddenly he came to a place where there were what seemed like inner and outer city walls and well-ordered houses, and in the distance he could see many weaver women in the palace. He saw a man leading oxen. . . . The [Sky Voyager] asked where [he] was. [The man] answered, "Go back . . . and put your question to [the astronomer] Yen Chün-p'ing; then you will know." In the end the [Sky Voyager] asked Yen Chün-p'ing, who said, "On a certain day of a certain month in a certain year a stranger star trespassed into the Draught Ox constellation." He calculated the year and month, and it was just when [the Sky Voyager] had arrived in Sky River.

Above: The Sky Voyager took a magical journey through the starry heavens.

A SPIRITUAL JOURNEY

The Monkey King

MANY MYTHICAL CHARACTERS HAVE SOUGHT IMMORTAL-ity, but none has done it with more flair than the Monkey King. This outrageous animal is the hero of a sixteenth-century CE novel called *Xi You Ji*, or *The Journey to the West*. The book is loosely based on the real-life pilgrimage of a monk named Xuan Zang, who journeyed to India to obtain the Buddhist scriptures for China. The fictional version of the monk's journey gives him three remarkable companions: a sand monster, a greedy pig, and the arrogant, adventurous, mischievous Monkey King.

Our retelling of *The Journey to the West* focuses on Monkey's early exploits, before the start of his westward journey. Following his miraculous birth, the bold little creature grows up to become the ruler of a monkey kingdom. One day he sets out to find the secret of eternal life. He becomes the disciple of a holy man who has attained immortality through mystical Taoist practices. Under this master, Monkey becomes an immortal and also gains supernatural powers. However, he remains a

Opposite: China's beloved Monkey King overcame all enemies through his courage, cunning, and trickery.

rascal. Leaving his teacher, he travels far and wide, causing turmoil with his irresponsible behavior. Not until he is brought before the Buddha himself does the troublesome character finally meet his match.

In some interpretations of this popular tale, the Monkey King represents human nature with both its virtues and its weaknesses. During his travels with the monk, he uses his powers to defeat monsters, help the helpless, and bring peace and order to the world. Through his courage, compassion, and devotion to duty, he makes up for the bad behavior of his early years and achieves true wisdom and enlightenment.

The Monkey King's story reminds us of the unique blending of faiths in ancient China. Although the plot of *The Journey to the West* revolves around the introduction of Buddhism to China, the characters achieve their victories largely through their Taoist powers. As Monkey tells a king encountered during their pilgrimage: "There is a Way in the Buddha's faith. . . . Combine the three teachings by honoring both the Buddhist clergy and the Way of Taoism, and by also educating men of talent in the Confucian tradition. I can guarantee that this will make your kingdom secure for ever."

CAST *of* CHARACTERS

Monkey King Famous trickster and hero
Yama King of the underworld
Dragon King Dragon ruler of the Eastern Sea
Yu Controller of the flood; last of the three Sage Kings
Jade Emperor Supreme ruler of heaven
the Buddha Founder of Buddhism
Xuan Zang Buddhist monk

The Search for Immortality

AT THE BIRTH OF THE WORLD, a stone egg appeared on a mountaintop beyond the Eastern Sea. For long ages the stone sat on its lonely peak, nourished by the sun, moon, and rain. One day it split open. Out popped a stone monkey. "Wonderful! Wonderful!" cried the funny-looking creature, and he scurried off to explore the world.

Now, all monkeys are playful, but this was the most cheerful, fun-loving creature the world had ever seen. He swung from the branches and splashed in the mountain streams. He made friends with the deer, wolves, leopards, and tigers. He led his fellow monkeys on so many

Monkey hopped aboard his boat and set off on a grand adventure.

merry adventures that they decided to make him their king. Ascending the throne, the stone monkey (who was not the most humble of fellows) gave himself a grand new title: Handsome Monkey King.

The Monkey King ruled over his subjects for three hundred carefree years. Then he began to worry about the future. "I am happy today," he said, "but one day Yama, lord of the underworld, will come to claim my soul. What is the point of being a king if I must be subject to that dread ruler's powers?"

So Handsome Monkey King made up his mind to find a master who could teach him how to live forever. He built a raft and drifted off into the great ocean. The winds carried him to a distant shore, where he saw his first people. He stole some clothes and swaggered about, imitating human speech and manners. Then he set off across the countryside. He wandered through towns and cities, barren deserts and thick forests. At last he found his way to the cave of an immortal.

The holy man agreed to accept the unusual-looking seeker as a disciple. Monkey stayed with his master for ten years, studying the Taoist scriptures and learning the way of immortality. He also learned how to perform many wonders. By the time he completed his studies, he could soar through the sky and change himself into seventy-two different forms.

> THE MONKEY KING FELT COMPLETELY AT EASE TO SOAR ON THE CLOUDS AND RIDE THE MIST.
> ⌐ THE JOURNEY TO THE WEST

Armed with his new skills, the Monkey King returned home, only to find his mountain kingdom in an uproar. A dreadful monster had robbed his subjects' homes and stolen their children! Roaring with anger, Monkey leaped into the air and somersaulted all the way to the lair of the monster. He used his magic to change the hairs on his body into thousands of little monkeys. The tiny creatures kicked, punched, poked, pinched, and pulverized the foul monster. Then Monkey gathered up the kidnapped children and flew them back to their delighted families.

After this glorious victory, Handsome Monkey King organized his subjects into an army. He armed his troops with swords, spears, battle-axes, and other weapons. But a great king and commander like himself could not use a mere earthly weapon. It was time to take another journey, this time through the water.

Reciting a spell and making a magic sign, the Monkey King parted the waters of the Eastern Sea. He strolled all the way down to the magnificent palace of the Dragon King. The dragon welcomed his immortal guest politely and offered him a variety of divine weapons. But Monkey had come for the scaly king's most valuable possession: the iron rod that Yu the Great had used to measure the depths of the oceans.

With his mighty powers, Monkey plucked the gigantic rod from the ocean floor. "Smaller!" he cried, and it turned into a tiny sewing needle. The mischievous monkey tucked the needle behind his ear. He helped himself to a priceless gold helmet and armor. "Sorry to have bothered you!" he called to the outraged dragon, and he leaped back out of the ocean.

A Journey to the Underworld

Handsome Monkey King strutted around his palace, showing off his treasures. He pointed out the polish on his new gold helmet. He made his iron weapon grow into a giant club and shrink back down to a little needle again. He howled with laughter as he described the way he had outsmarted the king under the ocean. "O Father," his awestruck subjects cried, "you are as great as the gods in heaven!"

But the real gods were not so impressed. That insolent ape was becoming a nuisance! It was time to put an end to his constant troublemaking.

The gods got their chance at a splendid banquet honoring the Monkey King's triumphs. The tables were piled high with delicacies, and the cups overflowed with wine. All the guests drank until they rolled off their seats to doze under the tables. While Monkey was snoring, two grim-faced men appeared. Without a word they tied up the king and dragged him down below the earth.

The hairy-faced prisoner reeled from side to side as his captors led him to the entrance of a city. Raising his head, he saw the sign above the gate: REGION OF DARKNESS. At that sight, Monkey was suddenly wide-awake and sober.

Yama's dreaded underworld kingdom was a place of torment and punishment.

"Why have you brought me here?" he cried. "The Region of Darkness is the domain of Yama, lord of death."

"We were given a summons to arrest you," the men grunted as they tried to haul their prisoner into the city.

Now Monkey was really angry. He whipped out the needle from behind his ear. *Whack!* His giant iron club reduced the two messengers to hash. He charged into the city, and all the demons and ghost soldiers fled at the sight of the fierce and angry warrior.

"Why did you send your men to arrest me? Don't you know that I am an immortal?" Monkey roared as he stomped into Yama's throne room.

The king of the underworld eyed the iron club nervously. "Many people have the same name. Perhaps there has been some mistake."

Monkey tapped his club against the floor, making the walls of the dark palace tremble. "Then get out your register of births and deaths, and let's see if we can fix this error," he growled menacingly.

Quickly the official in charge of the records produced the register. The Monkey King scanned the names until he came to this entry: "Soul number 1350. Heaven-born Stone Monkey. Age: 342 years. A peaceful death."

Monkey called for a brush and ink. He blotted out his name. He also crossed out the names of all his subjects. Throwing down the ledger, he shouted, "That's the end of my account! You have no power over me now!' Then the hairy-faced hero stormed out of the Region of Darkness.

The Hand of the Buddha

The Jade Emperor sat on his throne, nursing a dreadful headache. Complaints were coming in from the underworld, the Eastern Sea, and nearly every other part of the universe. He had to find a way to control that pesky Monkey!

At last the emperor came up with a plan. He would take advantage of the Monkey King's greatest weakness: his vanity. He would offer the rascal a small but important-sounding post in heaven, where he could keep an eye on him.

Monkey was thrilled when he received his appointment as Keeper of the Heavenly Horses. He rose to heaven on a cloud and proudly took up his duties. After a few days of mucking out the stables, though, he began to suspect that the job was not really such an honor.

So the Jade Emperor gave Monkey an even more impressive title: Guardian of the Garden of Immortal Peaches. The golden peaches that grew in this garden gave eternal life to all those who ate them. It took thousands of years for a new crop to ripen. When the fruit was ready, the gods and goddesses celebrated with a grand banquet.

The greedy Monkey King feasted on the peaches of immortality.

Feasting on the sweet, juicy peaches, they renewed their immortality.

As it happened, it was almost time for the banquet. Monkey longed for a taste of the ripe fruit that hung like balls of gold from the branches. He climbed up a tree and took a little bite. Delicious! He picked another fruit and ate it. One after another he gobbled up every single peach in the garden.

Monkey's crimes were soon discovered. The angry emperor condemned him to death for his wickedness. But the impudent character was doubly immortal now, and there was no way to kill him.

In desperation the Jade Emperor turned to the Buddha himself. The immortal master journeyed to heaven. He laughed when he heard about Monkey's antics. Taking the troublemaker into his hand, he asked, "Why do you keep causing a commotion?"

"I am Handsome Monkey King!" boasted the little fellow. "I am immortal. I can change into seventy-two different forms. One leap will take me thousands of miles through the air. With my superior powers, I should be the one sitting on the supreme throne of heaven."

"I will make a wager with you," laughed the Buddha. "If you can jump clear of my palm, I will ask the Jade Emperor to yield his throne. If not, you will go down to the earth and work harder to earn your immortality."

Eagerly Monkey agreed to the bargain. With one giant leap, he vanished into the clouds. He came down to earth far away, at the base of five tall pink pillars. Producing a magical brush, he wrote his name on the smallest pillar. Then he leaped into the air and soared back to where he had started.

"When are you going to begin?" asked the Buddha.

"What do you mean? I have flown to the ends of the earth and left a record of my visit. Would you like to go look at the place?"

> [THE BUDDHA] STRETCHED OUT HIS RIGHT HAND, WHICH WAS ABOUT THE SIZE OF A LOTUS LEAF.
> ⌐ *THE JOURNEY TO THE WEST*

"No need to go anywhere." At that, Monkey looked down and saw his name written on the base of the master's little finger. "You see," said the Buddha, "the whole world lies in the palm of my hand. No matter how far you fly, my hand is always beneath you."

And so the Monkey King was defeated. But his adventures had just begun. In the years that followed, he would travel to India with the great Buddhist monk Xuan Zang. During their long journey, the companions would encounter many obstacles and overcome many deadly perils. At last they would fulfill their mission, bringing the sacred Buddhist scriptures back to China. And through his faithful service, Monkey would achieve the greatest treasure of all: true enlightenment.

GLOSSARY

Buddhism the religion based on the teachings of the sixth-century BCE Indian wise man Siddhartha Gautama, known as the Buddha, or "Enlightened One"; the Buddha outlined a path of right conduct and understanding that would lead followers to a state of enlightenment

Confucianism one of China's ancient philosophies and religions, which developed from the teachings of the wise man Confucius, who stressed the importance of social order, morality, and the proper performance of religious rituals

culture hero a mythical hero and teacher who gives early humans the tools of civilization and helps them through his acts of courage and discovery

deities gods, goddesses, and other divine beings

divination a mystical practice used to communicate with the gods and spirits and discover hidden knowledge

dynasties ruling families who passed down their authority from generation to generation

A fierce god of thunder

enlightenment in Buddhism, the blissful state of total knowledge and freedom from desire

imperial relating to an emperor or empire

legend a traditional story that may involve ordinary mortals as well as divine beings and may be partly based on real people and events

mythology the whole body of myths belonging to a people

myths traditional stories about gods and other divine beings, which were developed by ancient cultures to explain the mysteries of the physical and spiritual worlds

Sage Kings three semidivine emperors who ruled over China during the Golden Age, a mythical period of perfect government; *sage* means "wise"

shape-shifter a supernatural being who has the power to change his or her body into different forms

steppes large treeless plains

Taoism (DOW-izm) one of China's ancient philosophies and religions, which teaches followers to live a simple life, in harmony with nature and the eternal principle of the universe, known as the Tao, or "Way"

trickster a mythical character who serves as a comical mischief maker, defeating enemies through his or her cleverness and trickery; tricksters can also be powerful culture heroes

yin and **yang** the two essential energies of the universe. Yin is dark, cold, damp, and submissive; yang is bright, hot, dry, and dominant. According to ancient Chinese beliefs, the constant interaction of these two opposing but related forces gives rise to the universe and everything in it.

The symbol for yin and yang

SOURCES *of the* MYTHS

The ancient Chinese passed down their myths orally for thousands of years. The oldest surviving written versions date back to around the fifth century BCE. These are mostly fragments of tales, mentioned in books on history, geography, philosophy, and other subjects. Over the centuries Chinese writers retold the old stories, interpreting them in different ways to illustrate their particular points of view. As a result, there are usually many variations of the same myth. The retellings in this book draw from a variety of sources, including the ancient texts described below.

Pangu the Giant and Nü Gua the Serpent Goddess

The earliest surviving accounts of Pangu, the giant who created heaven and earth, date back to the third century CE. Among these are two books written by a scholar named Xu Zheng: *Historical Records of the Three Sovereign Divinities and the Five Gods* and *A Chronicle of the Five Cycles of Time.* Xu Zheng may have adapted the Pangu myth from ancient stories that came to the Middle Kingdom from Tibet and central Asia.

The goddess Nü Gua is several centuries older than Pangu. She first appears in an important mythological document known as *Tian wen,* or "Questions of Heaven," which was written around the fourth century BCE. Over time the Nü Gua creation story gave way to the male-dominated myth of Pangu.

The Yellow Emperor

A large body of myths describe the battles of Huang Di, the Yellow Emperor. One of the most important written sources is *The Classic of Mountains and Seas.* This collection of hundreds of myths was written by various authors over a period stretching from the early third century BCE to the first or second centuries CE. Other major sources include *Huainanzi* ("Master Huai-nan"), compiled by Taoist scholars in the late second century BCE, and *The Annals of Master Lü,* from the third century BCE.

Yi the Archer and the Ten Suns

The divine archer Yi is one of China's most popular mythical heroes. Images of Yi shooting at the ten suns appear on a number of ancient tomb sculptures, and the story is mentioned in many myth-related texts. These include two major Confucian texts: *Analects*, a collection of Confucius's sayings compiled shortly after his death in 479 BCE, and *Mencius*, a record of the teachings of the fourth-century BCE Confucian scholar Mencius. *The Classic of Mountains and Seas* is also an important source for this myth.

Yu Conquers the Great Flood

No other Chinese character has inspired more myths, legends, and folktales than the hero Yu. The myth of Yu and the flood is found in numerous texts dating as far back as the middle Zhou dynasty. Major sources include: *The Classic of Poetry*, a collection of hymns and poems compiled around 600 BCE; *The Classic of History*, a mythological record of the deeds and speeches of the Sage Kings and other important beings; and *Records of the Grand Historian*, a 130-chapter book written by the first-century BCE historian Sima Qian.

The Weaver Maid and the Cowherd

This famous myth has been known and loved in China for centuries. The earliest known reference to the Weaver Maid dates back more than 2,600 years, to a poem in *The Classic of Poetry*. Later mythological texts began to link the goddess and the cowherd romantically. During the twelfth century CE, the historian Luo Yuan told the story in a book called *Er ya yi*, or "Material Appended to the 'Er ya [Dictionary].'" By that time, the myth had been filled out with details including the purpose of the

Weaver Maid's weaving, her identity as a star in the sky, and the reason behind the couple's tragic separation.

The Monkey King

The adventures of the Monkey King are recounted in *Xi You Ji*, or *The Journey to the West*. This famous novel was written in the late sixteenth century CE, probably by a little-known Chinese scholar named Wu Cheng'en. The book blends fact and fiction to tell the story of the real-life pilgrimage of the monk Xuan Zang, who journeyed to India in the seventh century CE and brought the texts of the Buddha's teachings back to China. The monk's most famous fictional companion was the Monkey King, also known as Sun Wukong, or "Enlightened Monkey." This mischievous character became one of the most popular figures in Chinese culture. Over the centuries Monkey's story has been retold in books, plays, operas, movies, TV programs, and cartoons.

To FIND OUT MORE

BOOKS

Ardagh, Philip. *Chinese Myths and Legends.* Chicago: World Book, 2002.

Collier, Irene Dea. *Chinese Mythology.* Berkeley Heights, NJ: Enslow, 2001.

Giddens, Sandra, and Owen Giddens. *Chinese Mythology.* New York: Rosen, 2006.

Helft, Claude. *Chinese Mythology: Stories of Creation and Invention.* Translated by Michael Hariton and Claudia Bedrick. New York: Enchanted Lion Books, 2007.

Kingsley, Rebecca, and Judith Millidge. *Chinese Gods and Myths.*

London: Quantum Books, 1998.

Roberts, Jeremy. *Chinese Mythology A to Z*. New York: Facts on File, 2004.

Sanders, Tao Tao Liu. *Dragons, Gods and Spirits from Chinese Mythology*. New York: Peter Bedrick, 1994.

Schomp, Virginia. *The Ancient Chinese*. New York: Scholastic, 2004.

Shone, Rob. *Graphic Mythology: Chinese Myths*. New York: Rosen, 2006.

Storm, Rachel. *Mythology of Asia and the Far East*. London: Southwater, 2003.

Storrie, Paul D., and Sandy Carruthers. *Yu the Great: Conquering the Flood*. Minneapolis, MN: Graphic Universe, 2007.

WEB SITES

The Big Myth at

http://www.mythicjourneys.org/bigmyth

> *The Big Myth* uses narration and flash animation to tell the creation stories of twenty-five cultures, including the ancient Chinese. You'll need to download Shockwave to view this entertaining site, which was developed for use in primary schools in Europe.

Encyclopedia Mythica: Chinese Mythology at

http://www.pantheon.org/areas/mythology/asia/chinese/articles.html

> This online encyclopedia offers more than 160 brief articles on Chinese gods, goddesses, and other mythical beings.

The Gods of Chinese Mythology at

http://www.godchecker.com/pantheon/chinese-mythology.php

> *Godchecker* is an online encyclopedia with a great sense of humor. The site includes a brief introduction to Chinese mythology plus lively articles on more than 150 gods and goddesses.

History for Kids: Ancient China at
http://www.historyforkids.org/learn/china/index.htm
> Explore the history, society, art, literature, and traditional beliefs of the ancient Chinese. This easy-to-read site is run by Dr. Karen Carr, Associate Professor of History at Portland State University in Portland, Oregon.

Internet Sacred Text Archive at
http://www.sacred-texts.com/world.htm
> The *Internet Sacred Text Archive* is an online library of texts on religion, mythology, and related topics, which have been scanned from the original books and articles. There are three China-related sections: "Buddhism," "Confucianism," and "Taoism."

Windows to the Universe, World Mythology, at
http://www.windows.ucar.edu/tour/link=/mythology/china_culture.html
> Created by the University of Michigan, this site gives visitors a choice of text presented at beginning, intermediate, or advanced levels. Here you'll find information and art relating to three of the mythical characters in this book: Pangu the giant (also called Pan-Ku); Yi, the divine archer who conquered the ten suns; and Yi's wife, the goddess Chang E (or Heng-O).

SELECTED BIBLIOGRAPHY

Allan, Tony, and Charles Phillips. *Land of the Dragon: Chinese Myth.* Alexandria, VA: Time-Life Books, 1999.

Birrell, Anne. *Chinese Mythology: An Introduction.* Baltimore, MD:

Johns Hopkins University Press, 1993.

———, trans. *The Classic of Mountains and Seas.* New York: Penguin, 1999.

Christie, Anthony. *Chinese Mythology.* New York: Peter Bedrick, 1985.

Editors of Time-Life Books. *What Life Was Like in the Land of the Dragon.* Alexandria, VA: Time-Life Books, 1998.

Ke, Yuan. *Dragons and Dynasties: An Introduction to Chinese Mythology.* Translated by Kim Echlin and Nie Zhixiong. New York: Penguin, 1993.

Leeming, David. *A Dictionary of Asian Mythology.* New York: Oxford University Press, 2001.

Loewe, Michael. *Everyday Life in Early Imperial China.* New York: Dorset Press, 1968.

Mackenzie, Donald A. *Myths of China and Japan.* New York: Gramercy, 1994.

Morton, W. Scott. *China: Its History and Culture.* 3rd ed. New York: McGraw-Hill, 1995.

Roberts, J. A. G. *A Concise History of China.* Cambridge, MA: Harvard University Press, 1999.

Shaughnessy, Edward L., trans. *I Ching: The Classic of Changes.* New York: Ballantine, 1996.

Werner, E. T. C. *Myths and Legends of China.* New York: Dover, 1994.

Yang, Lihui, Deming An, and Jessica Anderson Turner. *Handbook of Chinese Mythology.* New York: Oxford University Press, 2008.

Yu, Anthony C., trans. and ed. *The Journey to the West.* Vol. 1. Chicago: University of Chicago Press, 1977.

NOTES *on* QUOTATIONS

Quoted passages in sidebars come from the following sources:

"Nü Gua Repairs the Sky," page 41, from *Huainanzi*, in Anne Birrell, *Chinese Mythology: An Introduction* (Baltimore, MD: Johns Hopkins University Press, 1993).

"Chang E Escapes to the Moon," page 59, from *Chu xue ji*, in Anne Birrell, *Chinese Mythology: An Introduction* (Baltimore, MD: Johns Hopkins University Press, 1993).

"The Sky Voyager," page 75, from *Bo wu zhi*, in Anne Birrell, *Chinese Mythology: An Introduction* (Baltimore, MD: Johns Hopkins University Press, 1993).

INDEX

ABOUT *the* AUTHOR

VIRGINIA SCHOMP has written more than seventy titles for young readers on topics including dinosaurs, dolphins, occupations, American history, and ancient cultures. Ms. Schomp earned a Bachelor of Arts degree in English Literature from Penn State University. She lives in the Catskill Mountain region of New York with her husband, Richard, and their son, Chip.